Praise for *Inaccurate Histories*

"*Inaccurate Histories* is a rich reckoning with lineage, with life and death and dreams and sacrifice. In this collection, Versella is the empress of her own passion and pain, transforming lifeless fact into living lore."

—LINDSAY LERMAN, author of *I'm From Nowhere* and *What Are You*

"Reading Versella's newest collection is like looking at faded photographs or watching old home movies: the memories and lives are there, but incomplete: damaged and discolored by time and distance. Versella's poems are attempts at making sense of what ghosts stir behind that damage, primarily through the lives of generations of Italian and Italian-American women. Here, women are the keepers of domestic spaces and lineages, but more importantly, of secret knowledge. They are the mystics, the quiet backbones of families—they are the ones who endure, who remain. In these stunning poems, Versella traces the lives of women across time and continents, questioning what it means to be the ancestor of immigrants, to carry not only their blood, but their names—or lack thereof. Probing the histories and bloodlines of these women, Versella crafts a transporting narrative that will draw you in with its femininity that is as dark as it is divine."

—RAYE HENDRIX, author of *What Good is Heaven*

INACCURATE HISTORIES

INACCURATE HISTORIES

ALISE VERSELLA

2025

GOLDEN DRAGONFLY PRESS

AMHERST, MASSACHUSETTS

FIRST PRINT EDITION, January 2025
FIRST EBOOK EDITION, January 2025

ISBN: 979–8–9894116–4–1

Library of Congress Control Number: Requested

Printed on acid-free paper supplied by a Forest Stewardship Council-certified provider. First published in the United States of America by Golden Dragonfly Press, 2025.

For S.L.V
And 104 Seneca

Contents

"But I believed
the people in his stories really loved one another,
even when they yelled and shoved their feet
through cabinet doors or held a chair like a bottle
of cheap champagne, christening the wall,
rungs exploding from their holes.
I said it sounded harmless, the pomp and fury
of the passionate. He said it was a curse
being born Italian and Catholic."

EXCERPT FROM "FAMILY STORIES" BY DORIANNE LAUX

Filomena, Mildred, Angelina,
Alice, Michele

This is what the women do. Prepare the room.
Sweep the step—right to left, keep away the dead
Wash the linens in the tub and hang them on the line
Bring together with darning eye
Crocheted threads
Knead the bread. Knuckle to yeast and yeast to rise
Like the blood in our cheeks, the fire in our breasts
                              A conflagration in the stomach
We prepare the womb.

We alone bury our dead

                              Children

Keep our husbands'   secrets
Hold their violence

Become bronze statues—monolithic over stove tops
                              One day you will leave the stove on
Become a shade in your own house where you keep the blinds drawn

You will not cry when the husband dies you will wail –a strangled
    bird through the coal mine
And swallow the ash—you will not cry again
You will reflect on memory until the memory is shinier than how the
    rest of us lived it
                              You will mourn the present

We, women, ache somewhere deep
Tormented wraiths holding the walls of the house up
Tending to the living room of dying men

But we will love again

                         Children with cherub cheeks and Michelin thighs
We will dance again

Like seraphim with weary wings singing hymns above the fireplace.

La Strega, La Luna

Today the world is shrouded like
A veil Sicilian widows don to hide
The fact that they
Are not despaired
That their cruel sons
And abusive husbands
      Violent and greedy men
Fell
At the first sign of rebellion

For it was never the patriarch
Of a family to fear
It was the woman

She who stands to the side smiling
      Politely
Is far more capable of preventing
The entire world from collapsing

She will cool your dizzy head
With the palm of her hand—*Strega*
Before baking your crushed bones into bread

She will make love to you
And you will forget she isn't yours
Her eyes aren't quite right
When she tells you
She loves you
But you'll believe her
The same way you believe yourself faithful

That God could only exist as a man
And so you shame her
She is too much like the moon
Brings out
The beast in people
You call her crazy—*la Luna*

But today the world is shrouded
Like Mary in blue
And you cross yourself and shudder
At every shadow
Like you should.

Cleaning Ceremonies

I can't find the photographs my grandpa showed me last
Yet all his clothes still hang in this cramped closet
Like the cramped bathroom with the wheelchair
Still folded up in the corner
I light the sage on fire
In hopes of cleaning out old ghosts
Or maybe just the ghost of myself
       Watch the ashes dissipate out the window
Where that bumble bee buzzes like Jupiter in orbit
And I'm reminded of poor Pluto, no longer a planet
How Pluto was Goofy's dog and essentially my first real word
       Pointing at the Disney picture hanging in my nursery
I remember in kindergarten learning about the tongue
Where one would taste sour or sweet
And how much I hated bitter, dark chocolate
And it's all I can stomach now
Bitter chocolate and acrimonious coffee

My father's beard is prickly and I cried hysterically when he shaved it
Like how dare a zebra change his stripes on me like that?
I only date men with beards
       Shun the day they shave or trim it down
Whittle themselves away
Unceremoniously

I remember my grandpa's rosary
His white t-shirt and shaving cream
How soft and clean
To believe.

All I Hold in My Hands

Soft
Softly woman
There is still strength in the swath of soft skin collecting on the hips
How they housed the blood of your kin
There is still bite and sting left on these lips
That curled back to defend your right to speak
Quiet
Quietly woman
The earth won't end with a ruptured bang
It will snuff out without a show
      A candle flame
Pinched between forefinger and thumb
The deadliest predator in the jungle...
      You never hear them coming

You can break bones with a look
And you worry too much how you look
How somebody once said pretty paves the way
      When you don't have as much money as a man
Sweetly honey
Like sugar cane we cut
Off our hair
Like a lion without a mane
      Samson
Is he still as majestic without that course crown?
Why don't you look inside his jaw?
      Ask Delilah, that temptress, that jezebel
How can a woman be so powerful
As to bring a kingdom down?

Put your lipstick on
That war ready flag smiling to strangers on the street
No ugly words ever fell from my great-grandmother's tongue
But every holiday dinner
We would wait
For her arrival
The queen matriarch at the gate

I have always been told I have soft hands
Always surprised by my shake
Where did you learn to shake the hand of a man like that?
How smooth and cool
And firm
The way our teeth clip our words into short
       Digestible
              Phrases
Isn't my love easier to ingest like this?

Knowing
I am soft and quiet and sweet
Like my hands could never be that violent
That a woman could ever be
       Hard
              And loud
                     And bitter
You are a punk rock gospel
Woman
That music, that background noise they try to drown out
But you are the witch that would float
Walk across the water
Jesus
Scream hallelujah
Woman

Scream like a bird of prey
Who flew through the dark so silently
Until
She caught with her claws
The world.

I Think the Dead Are Watching Me

The glassy-eyed doe hung in the limbo of my living room
She hangs next to a wall of mirrors
In the mirrors I watch myself

She tells me, "It begins with the body
We are haunted by bones—their aching."

The skulls in my house are tattooed
With ink and pen and studded with garnet
There are
Stag horns and fox tails
Deer jaws
I clench my jaw so hard at night I feel like my teeth are decomposing

We save egg shells for composting
"Aren't we all made for the compost? Dear Whitman, bless this
compost."

The doe wants to unhook her mouth so I ask her, "Would you tell
me something soothing?"
She says, "Empty sockets are still seeing—a third eye type of
knowledge."

I say, "But I keep painting animals, my tiny little totems
And the eyes have no life to them
I cannot catch the glint."

Every morning, I walk down the hall, and the mirrored wall
Reflects me and the doe

"Do you still dream of pine-needled floors?" I ask her
As I stare at the glitter in the popcorn ceiling
And rub my eyes of sleep grit stars

I keep waiting for the doe eyelid (held perpetually open) to close
For my paintings to blink

For some ghost
To come awake
And tell me they're alive in a better place.

A Woman Holds a Vacancy

I am not my mother's firstborn.
An argument let
The bones of that skeleton
Tumble out of its closet

My mother's wound
A wounded baby bird
Starving in the nest
She is not the only one
To hold her secret in her chest

My mother's past life
Is the branch split by the lightning strike
Such thin skin on the newborn bird
I notice as it lies crushed in the dirt

My mother's remaining children and her ghosts haunting the room.

The unspoken hollows in the family tree
My grandmother's wounded womb
A hysterectomy
A piece of her removed
A woman would
Carve out her organs until emptied
To feel forgiven the heavy
Stones of the dead son she buries
No photography
To immortalize a memory

A mother's remaining children and the ghosts haunting the room.

Mother, every year you swallow the moon
And a new crater is carved out of you

I know of the craters formed
In women who yearn
My aunt who wished her womb could do more
Was told by the doctors a pregnancy
Would cause more harm
To her already ravished insides

A woman's only child and the ghosts haunting the room.

Mother, you are planet and gravitational pull
A daughter is the satellite that orbits you
Do not think her devoid of light
If her galaxy never breeds stars

Somehow I decided
My belly would never be full
A deflated, uterine balloon
A vacancy, but no one could rent the room

I am not incomplete
If you tie up the tributaries
That run through me

I will have no firstborn
There will be nothing to bury or mourn
I will overflow in other ways

A woman remains, exorcising the ghosts from the room.

This Time Tomorrow

Yesterday
Will be like the plastic that collected dust on your couch

You
Will evaporate
Same as the rain
From the asphalt in August

You
Become the living room organ
Transplanted in a dying forest

What we become as we grow through the days…

This day
Is nothing less than a gift

That the body would greet you again
With a different sigh

This time tomorrow you will be different
But how holy
That a ghost never forgets the memory of its body.

No One Covered the Fig Tree

Italians wrap their fig trees in burlap for winter
Like my mother wrapped us in her grandmother's crocheted sweaters
I hated the sweaters
And the coats my great-grandmother would buy me for Christmas
Like I was on display—something to be approved of
She didn't approve
of my blue nail polish, still I choose blue at the nail salon most days.

Italians grow gardens; we took the roots in our suitcases overseas
Meaning: a non-native species can learn how to flourish where it is
planted
As long as it is tended to lovingly
We moved away, and I had no choice but to grow somewhere that
never felt like home
Home being the houses boxed up and sold
Who knew I'd miss that Christmas coat as I grew old?

Each year, I long for approval from someone
To tell me I'm doing it right—the garden, no, I mean life
I want credit for flourishing despite the cold
Sometimes Italians will bury the fig tree for winter
But I've already buried so many trees in my family
I can't bend my limbs into their soil anymore

This summer we got too much rain
So the fruit dropped, too heavy
Rotted in the grass
What becomes of the fig and the fig milk's stain?
What becomes of the roots after the tree is cut down and the stump
Is all that remains?

Mother

She's spent a lot of time hiding herself in junk drawers
With dead batteries and loose buttons and mismatched cutlery and
    unpaired chopsticks
All the old mustard packets from the takeout boxes her first night in
    this house
The same house you grew up in
Cried over broken hearts in
She always told you buck up, they weren't worth crying over
And you just wanted to cry harder on her shoulder
She must've cried in private
That first time you called her a cunt
She must have
Doubted her title, her ability, to do anything right for you
They do give up their life for you
The parts you are just now experiencing—the freedom of your body
Hers isn't hers anymore
It ceased where it's dimpled, congealed into divots, sagged and wrinkled
She's transferred breath to you
Blood raging every month just so you could grow up
Bloom where you are planted
Root sturdy enough to become transplanted
And thrive
In richer soils, more spacious
Gardens
A garden of your own
She lives for you now
Do you understand that kind of responsibility?
You may call it pressure
Like how can you possibly

Measure up
But she calls it love
And no matter what
To her you will always be enough.

Memory's Wretch

As I count the exits from Nassau to Queens
I think back to that time stuck in traffic on the BQE
And how desperately you needed to pee
How the firehouse bathroom was the cleanest you'd ever seen

We were going to the Museum of Natural History—prehistoric
     creatures in a prehistoric city
Architecture as old as some bones and reminiscent of past aesthetics
     of opulence and ornateness
You wanted to be an architect, I wonder if it makes you bitter that
     you didn't

Steel towers scissor open the sky, slice through sunlight
Open up snapshots of memory that skitter through Manhattan's avenues

Like a loosened candy wrapper from a lime green lollipop that one
     Halloween…
The smell of asphalt reminding me always of metal slides and rubber
     swings
                                        Grandpa in the park
               Grandpa as we got stickers in the drugstore
As we picked up the newspaper at Miggy's
Raisinets and York Peppermint Patties on the conveyor belt
Fresh Italian bread for sandwiches at every visit

Sleepovers and the scent of grandma's night cream, grandpa's skin
     after shaving
His nighttime bathroom rosary

Those beads lay on my dresser now, as does her lipstick—it
    still smells like her kisses
I am full of wishes to once again watch my sister napping on their
    couch after lunch
To pick cherry tomatoes and string beans in his garden
For a salad we'd spin in bowls I now hold in my own apartment
To spend the afternoon pretending I know how to play that old organ
The sweaty stick of bare thighs on plastic-covered furniture and
    afternoon pie
    "You want that à la mode? You want that à la mode."

The onslaught of these memories is replete with the underpinnings of
    joy under grief:
Looking in her bedroom mirror preparing for his funeral, *Band of
    Horses* playing in my head.

How many memories we lose with our dead
No one left to reminisce with but the two of us

The crispness in the air today, ginkgo leaves plastered to the sidewalk
And church bells ringing *Amazing Grace*
Remind me of you
For a moment, melancholy modifies the colors sunset makes of this
    island
My home is away from you now
And I wrack the rolodex of memories I have to keep you close
Promising to call and make time to visit, steal all the time I can
Before memory is all I have

How sweet that sound of memory
That saves the grieving.

Abraham's Antonym

My father did not have sons, he had daughters
He raised to be strong women
Maybe stronger than the men
He knew who went to prison
Who got into bar fights at motorcycle clubs

My father gives the best damn hugs
Few and far between
Like the absence of them makes them all the more glorious
When you receive one
My father is the strongest son
Of a bitch
And that woman had the tiniest fists
She didn't put up with her husband's shit
My father taught me to take no man's bullshit

I will crush you between my teeth
My smile is jagged and the mountain of my body steep
You will trip over me and the world will call it accident
Never for a moment doubt
The intentions of a beautiful woman
Protecting her territory with her feet

Jesus didn't save me
But Saint Michael of South Beach did
When he taught me how to fall
From grace
And get back up again
That no matter how often I fall

You always get back up
And my face is the first thing protected
Hands out to fend off the world
This face is the last best thing you will see before the lights go out
Knockout

I am the holy lightning in this darkness
My father did not have sons
So he taught his daughters how to light up the dark
And I am not terrified
Of the creatures that lurk
In that night
My father taught his daughters how to fight

Because daughters remember that the world owes them nothing
So they must always be clawing
At their dreams

I have grabbed onto every star that fell in a meteor shower
Until the scalding little deaths burned my flesh
This is how I get closer to the moon
This is how the daughter wins

And my father's laughter fills up the room
You never knew laughter to sound so good
My father has daughters who laugh harder than you
We laugh when we want to cry and the laughter keeps us alive
We are the daughters who lit up every pitch-black sky
And gave you some god to believe in.

Store Brand Numerology

There are bars of halva at the deli counter
I like to pull our ticket
The older I get, the more obsessed I become with numbers
For the lottery, you play our birthdays, your old badge number
Each numeral some sort of sign
I wait in the deli line
Get used to free slices of American white

I think about the bars of halva
And the halves of you and me   Strands of time, our DNA
Sitting on the bench under her fig tree
You placed me in the branches like a bird
There are places, nests in my memory
Where, like migratory birds, I keep returning

I want the peeling bark to mean something
The numbers on the counter counting for more
Than ¼ lbs of store-brand meats
The expensive things
We can't afford
You tell me, "not today" as a way
To keep hope alive in the grocery store

An old boyfriend said the halva tasted like chalk paste
I disagreed and said it was a sweet treat—a delicacy

Memory makes the taste seem richer-like luxury
And I lacked nothing

I stand at the deli line and the number I pull seems lucky.

To the Woman Who Said She Liked My Necklace

After Sara Borjas

I said something about how lucky
We are to have cars
To take us to the corner grocery store

How we
Have air-conditioning
And a floor fan
You still use 'cause you're afraid the cold will run out

Still sweating the memory of Sunday Dinners with roaches in corners
    and Tar Beaches burning

My great-grandmother clutched her—"*balige*" like other women
    clutch their pearls
Close to the neck
I think my great-grandmother could've wrung a man's neck
If she had to
We women, have to learn how to do things we normally wouldn't
    want to
Out of necessity

It is necessary
To state
This gold necklace was the only treasure they could afford
So when I think about grocery stores
And suburbia
How much I scorn small-town America
I really meant to say thank you
I know how much it cost to get out.

Apollo

You will swim out to the Verrazano
To test virility with your brother, Carlo
While records play opera like a chorus of sparrows

You will search for meaning in Montana, become the son that follows
His father's secrets and sorrow, bring home no answers, only crystals
You will swim out to the Verrazano

You will send an uncle to Vietnam, and the world will narrow
Like arteries in your heart and our heartbeats echo
While records play opera like a chorus of sparrows

You will build a home in a suburban city borough
Rats on the beach and bodies under boardwalk rubble
You will swim out to the Verrazano

You will leave behind pain for the rest of us to swallow
When I was a baby, my mother thought she saw your shadow
While records played opera like a chorus of sparrows

Your memory becomes the arrow
Shot through our lineage and into tomorrow
You will swim out to the Verrazano
While records play opera like a chorus of sparrows.

Coffee Breaks and Familial Aches

The day
Is frenetic energy
Neutrons bouncing in a nucleus—the walls of this
Kitchen
I stop to percolate
Filter the day through me like water through the coffee beans

Café
Bustelo takes me back
To a particular time of day
The way
My father takes
The Sambuca
To an espresso cup, much too small for his callused and arthritic
hand
Places a twirl of lemon curl
Wet around the rim and drops it in

The bitter bite, a harpoon
To drown the day's demons down
His nerve-damaged spine, slackening
Back relaxing
My father, captain, loud at the helm
Rendered
Quiet
For a few hours in the afternoon

Most days, we circumnavigate the globe of his moods
Each coffee cup or shot glass, a different port

Heaven Hill after an argument
Two cups of coffee or three
Depending
On the previous night's sleep

My father does not sleep
Years of shift work
Shifting the meridians
Of his body

Most children
Think themselves polar opposites
Of their parents
But I am finding
The coffee is staining my teeth
It becomes harder and harder for me to fall asleep
Is this predisposition
Hereditary
This need for bitter comfort,
Mercy?

The espresso
an expression
A confession
Because I did not go to catholic school
Cannot recite a Hail Mary
But I am full of grace
In this caffeinated state
Café Bustelo, salvation
As the scent of it fills my nostrils

For a moment I breathe deeply
And relax, like my father, into the warmth of the sun

Streaming in through the
Kitchen window
On a hectic afternoon.

Smoked Herring for Breakfast

The rattan-backed chair is splintering
Splitting
Like my hair. You find a strand of it in the meal I prepared

I've disappointed you

So many times in this kitchen
I want to blame you for everything. But it was me
Only me
Who broke the dinner plate
On my big toe after washing

The cutlery is beginning
To remind me of metacarpals and phalanges
I'm holding the finger bones of your dead friends
And they haunt our filet and the spinach leaves
Shriveling with the boiling

The last time I grated parmesan at the restaurant
I made a ribbon of my thumb
Felt the blood drum beat of my throbbing flesh and thought
What a lovely dress
My soul wears

The last time he was over
We couldn't find the corkscrew to dislocate the wine he drank too
   much of
He never complimented my dress

My mother concocts coffee as a milky cocktail each morning
And I bristle at the scent of nutmeg in biscuits
Two teaspoons too many is poisonous
Or possibly
Hallucinatory

I've never had smoked herring
But I feel that it's what I'm becoming
Dried out and my body, laid over the coals, takes on a reddish tint

My valuable flesh drowning in the shallow waters of its home

I've heard rumors, that wild herring spend their whole life trying not to
    be eaten
And I've spent my whole life cooking the kitchen a sufficient meal of
    my meat

Day breaks and I wake
To bury the burnt fish in the ground.

Only in Dreams Now

I dreamt of you again
        That you were both together makes me believe in a Heaven
Something warmer and more loving than the chaos here
The tornado that twists through the house
Blows through the rib cage
Severs something new each time

I reached for you
And I woke for the first time with the realization
No one is reaching back
The ache becomes vaster
The farther the valley of the past
Deepens
The mouth of the cave widens
It feels like it will devour what's left of who remains
I long to hear him laugh again
With me
Share an album over Bustelo with Sambuca and a lemon rind
Time
Wrinkles our eyes
Sadness digs in and bitterness
We hollow
The dream is the only place I find them now
The family and the comfort
Oh, how I long to wake and be comforted
By the breakfast we share
But we remain
Silent

We stare at our plates and speak no more
The cavern widens
The father goes in
The daughter can no longer find him.

Anger Is a Lightning Storm

You're electricity—a katana through the sky
And I am not a gifted swordsman
Much better at wielding the wind
Tree branches of druid oaks
Somehow never cracking
But the bark, it sure is singed

The wires surging
Hurt
Each split end whipping wildly
Sparking in the dirt
The water is mostly salt
Disappointment and regret

For arguments
Between parent and child
The storm is a rhinoceros
A stampede of black clouds
And poisoned sediment
All the roots exposed
And crumbling from the garden bed

The bed is drowned
The flowers, dead
The electric needles the sky
Like the faded tattoo on your shoulder
I can no longer read our names
Now that we've grown older
The tree strains against the wind.

Cerebral by Nature

My father plays his life like a chess game
Four steps ahead to outmaneuver you
      My sister beats him every time
Moves her queen to c4
They are the same you see
Internally battling some demon unseen

I don't have the patience for chess
Ransack the board with the quickest offense
I react first –like my mother
Deal with the consequence later
        Or never
Denial looks most beautiful when all its pieces are spread out against
  the table

On this table we hold no salt
We never look back long enough
      To become pillar
Deflect with knight and castle, offer holy bishop casualty
A memory of my father so angry, he flipped the kitchen table

My mother broke every vase
           We don't hide our feelings inside ceramic anyway

But it took forever to move every pawn across the board
And retrieve the pieces we had lost

She slapped my mouth once
And my teeth bit lip drew from it

Blood
I ran through the street barefoot

A chess game can be as chaotic
Especially when played in my house
Each move becomes metaphor for underlying truths
There is no winner in a stalemate
But most times, one of us is simply holding out

The only lesson I've learned from chess
Has been how not to quit
For all our shit, never underestimate my family
We can play this game all day...we invented it.

Beauty Mark or Blemish

My sister and I
Share the same freckle on our right hand
Sound the same on the telephone and sometimes
Shy away from what we know is better for us
Perhaps we think we don't deserve much
A little damaged by the family that raised us
Searching for the parallel lines that would take us to a brighter
    finish line

She was the first to catch a fish on that taut line
We spent our summers pulling up crab cages in the Pines
Learned our father's favorite curse word, "Mother…"

She no longer touches tequila
I no longer have the effort for rage
Worn out and trying desperately
To hold on to happiness in an unhappy place

She is always persevering
The only one of us committed to the shipbuilding
I spend a lot of time forgetting
That I used to roll white bread balls in sugar because I read it in a
    book once
That I am just as much
From Ireland as Italy and famine isn't always related to the stomach
We are tender-hearted sisters
Ragtag and hasty but innovative and brazen
Engineers of our own survival

I didn't mean to abandon you in the lake
To the dark and waste
I used to think our futures were prearranged

I had no choice but eavesdropping on our parents; brittle walls and
    tiny halls
Pleasure and violence
Did you hear what I heard, see what I saw?
Behind closed doors or
That night in the living room-brawl on the couch
Did it strip you of something like it did to me?

I remember you coming into my bed when the dog seized,
How you didn't want him to die
And I still don't know how to comfort you, how to make the
    horrible truths
Less a chisel that cuts away at you

We mounted horses in the woods one day
We never felt so free…

Inaccurate Histories

Maybe my great-grandparents didn't take a steamer trunk and head to Ellis Island to eat pasta with cockroaches in a four-story walk-up in Harlem with no air-conditioning

Maybe the only heaviness my great-grandmother had to carry from the bus up the flights of stairs were her rubies and emeralds and diamonds and pearls and not the groceries

Maybe my great-grandpa had a happy family with a mother and father and he knew his real last name, wasn't dropped off on the doorstep of some family friend, never to speak of that family again

Maybe he didn't run booze and cheat at cards or eat rats while imprisoned fighting another man's war

Maybe this is all a farce and I wasn't born in the middle of a swamp with mafia at the corner of the streets with the little white house and Ambrose's candy store

Maybe I was born into more

There were no bodies buried under the boardwalk boards, the beach was clean, the sand was white, nobody contracted AIDS and died

I didn't grow up

I didn't grow up

I made this all up

There is no family straining against the nooses of their history

There is nothing leaking from the roof

There is nothing breaking.

A Family Is the Suit of Swords

The Cedar trees of which my street is named for
Are greying all around me
Their leaves browning, burning

A family on fire and we are choking
On the smoke from the myrrh from my grandpa's Catholic, funeral
   mass
The wind chimes sound like they are singing
Death's dirge—a warning to the still living

I find no strength in this kyanite
The shards pierce the pale blue bruises

The owl in the tree keeps shrieking
That Themis's scales are weighed unevenly
With kidney stones

A blockage where the Tigris once flowed freely
The three of swords means suffering
And we are suffering greatly
Counting our ten swords of betrayal
Four warriors soldiering on
And not one of us willing

To let go of the knife.

Perhaps the World Ends Here

After Joy Harjo

The thread starts under the needle
Of my grandmother's Singer Sewing Table
No matter that I cannot sew
One must first
Begin.

Guilt feeds these threads, instructing each stitch
My foot taps the pedal
We progress, inch by inch.

I recall the day my dog caught a chipmunk in his maw
(The needle catches my skin)
I think he felt only joy
(Each zipper I see sewn is a row of biting canines).

This machine has closed the holes and tears
Time wove into a rag-doll
Reattached the button eyes
Sewed shut the spewing stuff
Unspooling from her insides

This machine
Has been operating table, altar, and sometimes grave
And one might feel like a god with a scissor
Snipping the loose threads of fate

I enact a burial for the unused scraps
Of fabric
Too inadequate

To patch the bitter memories
Nostalgia's ghosts keep unraveling

I am trying
To sew a satchel full of lavender
All the while remaining
The Tarot's favorite Fool as the spools rapidly keep turning

The world will end here
When the last stitch is removed from the wound
The scar no longer raised and red
But pale constellation,
The echo of my brief scream in the night.

The Cup Runneth Over with What?

What spills over seeps into the cloth
Every drink poured
Generation to generation, I sop it up

Dry the mess from the Formica table
Dry the well that pools on the ledge of the cheeks,
The counter space and the dripping sink

My great-grandfather poured whiskey in his coffee every morning
    until the day he died
Cheated at cards and ran booze for the mob
My father takes a shot
Sometimes to sleep. I noticed the bottle on the countertop
After endless arguments
Where our dog would sit shaking in the corner of the laundry room
He made his bed.
My father sleeps on the couch most nights because night shifts in the
    prison
Shifted something in him.

My mother broke a lot of vases back then.

My grandpa would pour Ovaltine into milk for me and I think he
    hated my father
And maybe his father too, at times
Both violent, angry men with women who grew silent making
    excuses for their husbands

Often, I have been tempted to pour gin into my tea
If my body is a vessel
Does what gets poured into this glass
Ever make room for the bubbles of air
Am I ever weightless? Relieved of the liquid density flowing under
    the skin of my wrists

The oil and vinegar is always said not to mix
But we spin olive and balsamic in the bowl until it's glorious
Over the salad in the wooden bowls we use to dine on our family
    traumas

I try to choke down the tougher meat; the stew is not always a sweet
    thing
Sometimes, it feels like lead in the belly
But at least I didn't go to bed hungry

I swallow what has been given to me
Thank them like the drink is holy sacrament, the only way to be
    absolved of my history
So I can tie the burst pipe with the shirt off my back
Dry the rivers of the past before it floods the room

I am careful with what I choose
To fill my cup with now
Pour flutes full of bubbles for all my friends
Give them air
Nothing dark enough to spill, leaving stains on their carpets

When a liquid reaches its boiling point
It just evaporates.

Amatulli

My mother has strong wrists
I know this
Because she whisks batter and dough better than any machine

My great-grandma Gugliemini
Broke the necks
Of chickens with her bare hands, hands that scrubbed the laundry in
    a tub for seven kids

My grandma Versella chose metal after she broke the wooden spoons
    and then she got the boots
Sent them flying through the air like pigeon wings
My father refusing to go to school

Grandma muttered *"shit"*
And *"Gesu Crist!"*
A woman with the side of her palm caught between her teeth

They traded in their maiden names and I think
Of all the things I am asked to give away
What kind of life would be given to me in exchange?

I do not know my great-grandma Guglielmini's maiden name
It faded, like her voice in my memory
I don't remember how it sang

My grandmothers wed savage men but were granted the peace of
    outliving them
I watched their hands, slender fingers unadorned
Nails painted vermillion

My mother taught me how to whisk egg whites for my life
Stiff peaks as she treated me to strong coffee and Turkish Delights
She taught me second helpings

To take what I want and give away nothing
So I grab the fruit fallen off vine from the floor
And reach towards each branch for more

These persimmon trees that grow between
The sidewalks on Seneca and Appleby
I pile their offerings up like loot

I wait for the fruit to just about rot
     The best tasting dowry,
Before I squeeze the sweet flesh from its skin into my mouth.

Dustsceawung

(The contemplation that dust used to be other things...the walls of a city...dust is the ultimate destination...)

The avenues are swollen
Trash fluttering like aerialists
Women wringing their wrists
  The bus late, again
Flatbush and Staten Island sweats
Corrupts, entraps us
With their glorious scent
  Warm summer asphalt, fresh laid
  Basketball rubber and hoop chain effigies
We lazily watch the ceiling fan
Desperate for air
Giggle in spite of the heat or maybe because of it
  Delirious with a fervor only two little girls could have in this
    brief night of summer
The texture of it heavy with weather
Static-y like the fuzz crackling on the TV, crackling like ginger ale...
  Every night we stayed Grandma would grab cans of it from
    the basement
  The side door opened to screen to let in any semblance of a
    late summer breeze
  Aunt and uncle on the front stoop, his and hers cigarettes
  Sneaking salt water taffy from Jersey...
My favorite ocean is this prairie of high-rises
The heights of hopeful dreams before the building foreclosures
Before the city comes toppling down all around us with
 September's rubble

Burning like fall leaves in gutters and the sirens singing change
    their tune
I want to remember this sweet perfume: Late August, nicotine,
And Revlon lipstick rimming the can of ginger ale left on the counter
    by the sink
Grandma puts us down to sleep
Window open to the sounds of late night on the expressway
Goethals to Verrazano
Horns and roaring engines, poker game laughter
Cigarette ash like dust on the kitchen table
Look at the city we had built for us
How they placed it in our hands
The condensation gathers on the can
I stare at my hands.

Home Is a Fig Tree

Home is the fig tree
It's hug of bark scratchy
Like the sweaters she'd quietly crochet
The leaves nip at my cheeks
Like a grandmother's lipstick staining greeting

Home is where I received
My first cut, the swift bleed,
       Red like the tricycle
Gravel pockmarking my knee
The stinging salt and the asphalt
A grandfather's hands and the Band-Aid

Home is where our champagne eyes fizz in the night
Like the sparklers you gave us on the fourth of July
And we spelled out our names on Seneca
Effervescence through the
Pepsi Cola dark
Until we believed ourselves golden
The homemade spark
Of fireworks
Set off in a backyard on Appleby
Little girls and tootsie rolls trying to be
Grown up

Home is the hum electric
The window unit and traffic
The booming laughter
Down the hall

The cigarette smoke
Blackjack kings and aces
I still remember their faces…

The silence at that table now
Vibrates so loudly it echoes.

The Sexiness in the Heat of Summer

These days come fast and hot

The humidity clutches to my insides—fills up my lungs

I have to remind myself to breathe most days

Deeply

The   stop-and-look-up-at-the-sky-notice-the-grass-beneath-you-take-note-of-the-flower-and-the-dragonfly-and-the-new-wrinkles-in-your-father's-face-deeply

I have to tear my eyes away from screens

Unless they are the window kind—collecting dew or the summer rain in their tiny little squares

I run my fingers across them like a Spanish güiro

There is a longing in this heat to dance

To run my hands over my hips and spin wildly in the street—a salsa

To get closer to each other

Close like I am kneading bread—pushing holes into focaccia, filling them up with salt water

I want to taste the salt on your lip

I want to catch the sweat that drips between my breasts like I am young and still searching the dark for lightning bugs—running and halting after each flicker and fade out

I want the heat aflame beneath my cheeks like a revolution

How breathing is hard here but the rapid inhale sounds like

Victory

How the scorched earth slides into a cool mosquito breeze like the exhale after climax—the release

After holding in all the tension

The moon and its foggy haze, a jaundiced glow

A stable direction, like how you know the way home without them

Instinct

The swell of this season, a sea in my bottomless belly thrashing boats to shipwreck

But I have batten down my hatches in this storm

And after every bellow of thunder and lightning shriek, the green tinge in the sky looks like acrylic cans poured down from the heavens

Most days, I wake reaching back towards dreaming, how I crave everything the world told me I couldn't have

How every morning it is just within my grasp—blurred along the edges

If I could only stay here a little longer, tug the line a little harder

I would catch that monster

These days are a tug-of-war

Muscles heaving beneath their skin

To run

Like roots uplifting through the tar—the congealing ink we pour again and again steams in the sun like our boiling blood

They say the Italian girls have hot blood

Oh, how we rage

Our little bodies a violent ray of heat—we love like we burn

Blistering

Tomato skins peeling away on the vine

Bursting delicious in the mouth

These days are a delicacy I want to move my tongue around—how it explores sensation

Savoring

Would that I could savor your sweet-bitter mouth, your salt-tang and acidic teeth

That you would smile and lie back in the sun

These days, I turn my face up and stare directly

Into the sun

Things I've Heard While Growing Up Italian

"You don't look I-talian."
"Do you get dark in the summer?"
"Do you know anyone in the mob?"
"Of course she's Italian, she's from Staten Island."
"And look at her nose…"

Yes let's address my Romanesque
Nose
That hooked beak
For so many years I loathed
My profile
Learned the perfect head tilt, the proper way to smile

Do you know my great-grandparents came outta Harlem?
Yes 110th
Do you know I can't
Say anything nice in their native tongue

But boy do I know how to eat
And I can feed you well
Take a look at this meat
This Sunday bread

This superstitious Catholicism
I cross my chest
        There are a lot of names I won't take in vain

Instead
I think about the blood of my father's
        Father's
Father lush within my veins
It's a stain that blooms
Roses throughout the carpet
You can't rinse the blemish
Of a created name
But what is a name
Except a mark of one's history?

Greasy Guinea

I still have the steamer trunk they came with off the boat
Seems unfit that one's whole life could hide inside of it

My mother's job at the stock exchange. They didn't like her name.
She hid behind *married*
They didn't care that *Guglielmini* means "little William"

People ask why I get so pissed when they miss the proper pronunciation
Of my name
Can never guess that this mess of letters in a foreign alphabet would
    mean so much to me
At least they didn't say, "hey bitch"

But I have lived for years within this name and heritage
Have grown accustomed to defining myself by the looping l's that swell
Off my tongue when I tell you it's *Versella*

My last name is a verse of poetry
A tree that extends its roots through the city
And connects the constellations like a street grid
A subway map home

Yes, I am Italian
A vivacious, passionate woman
I know what it is to live
Because we are always dying
Like a language you can no longer recall
The olive-skinned faces of grandfathers' long gone

I am holy divinity carved
From marble
The grace in a Renaissance painting
The Madonna as you pray for salvation
Yes I am indeed, Italian

As golden and blood as oil and wine
And I taste just as sweet on the tongue.

The Old Block

After Ras Heru

He asked us to, "Picture your block."

Myblockmyblockmyblock

           I don't have one.

My block has been disappearing, like the fig trees and the grandfathers who knew how to tend them.

Little Italy used to be fifty blocks and now it's three, a tourist destination with over-priced chicken parm instead of a neighborhood, fully functioning. In the early twentieth century, more than four million Italians immigrated to the island of Manhattan, splitting themselves between Mulberry Street and East Harlem. My great-grandparents settled at 78th street—a four story walk up and no air conditioning, roaches dining with the aunts and uncles on Sundays. They came here with a steamer trunk that now sits in my living room, filled with the crocheted blankets in cheap brown yarns—all the darning's of a dream.

> They dreamed the dream of golden pavement and opportunity and they got it, moving to outer boroughs and later the shores of Jersey, didn't they? Didn't we make it, in this new country, four generations later, staring at the burning world and all its blazing glory?

I watched them hold their tongues, learn a new language, forget the old one. Turn the other cheek at "Greasy Guinea"

"Savage"
  "Dago"
    "WoP."

My language is disappearing. "I can't say anything nice in my native tongue…" learned all the bad words first. The words have all been bastardized I mean *Americanized. Goomba, gabagool, gidrool…*

I think the destruction of a language happens first. The easiest way to destroy a culture after you bulldoze its universities, its hospitals, kill their poets, slash the art. Tell them, "Speak English!" Shout it at them until they crawl inside their olive skin and never speak it again in front of their children, in front of their grandkids.

Assimilate stunad

Until the dark skin they lynched in New Orleans bleaches like bones in the sun

Until you forget you're notorious for violence so you lose your backbone, bend your spine

        Stay silent so your voice doesn't ripple their streams

Forget your faith.

My friend went to Kansas and the woman asked him if he was "One of them I-talians," was he "Catholic?"

A religion steeped in superstition, silly little rituals. (America was mostly Protestant in the early 1900s and just like the Irish, devout Catholicism didn't fit *American Ideals*)

Our families of eight in tenements were not ideal either—my great grandmothers and their washboards, their hands breaking chicken necks and kneading bread, walking blocks with bags of groceries their granddaughters still can't afford, but we make do anyway. Stretch and stretch <I scrape the bottom of every jar until there's no scrap left> until we are tall, head held high and shoulders back

Something resembling proud.

Proud of my heritage, proud of the endurance of generations that brought me here: strong willed and maybe a little bit unforgiving.

Maybe one day I will forgive America her bullies but I cannot forget them

They, who couldn't be damned to spell correctly our names at Ellis Island so we just made them up, I guess Versella was good enough. Our names you mocked, you glorify now your Tony Soprano, your Cousin Vinny, but never my Grandpa Vito, my uncle Nunzio, my uncle Salvatore.

They, who deemed us ruthless and dishonest, criminal, never gave us a fair trial. Say Maria Barbella, say Sacco, say Vanzetti. And in their prejudice they rounded 418 of us up to Missoula, Montana as *enemy aliens* and on October 12, 1942 deemed us worthy of appeasement, no longer a threat to national security, so they gave us the statue of a man who stole indigenous land and we were supposed to say thank you, thank you for finally considering us worthy of dignity.

I am indignant. That cultures can assimilate to the point of disappearing that nothing melded in this so called melting pot and the tar they melted over the dirt on old city blocks is asphalt I no longer recognize. It is happening everywhere I turn my eyes. They gentrify everybody's neighborhood and call it growth, "Be mesmerized by all this wealth you cannot touch."

They turn us against us.

We say to one another, "You're not Italian enough, not Sicilian enough," I don't speak the language right or practice the old traditions, I've never stepped foot in Italy. But I'm learning, trying to regain something my ancestors were forced to lose.

So many of us feel that too.

I felt it when he asked us to picture our blocks, the places our families immigrated to, how a new generation of us are left with *diaspora* but no place left to scatter to. That's what it means diaspora in ancient Greek, to scatter about. To scatter from your homeland across the globe and spread your culture as you go. It should be beautiful, to share your culture, but we make it ugly don't we? Turn down our noses and shun what is *other*. Shove it into ghettos and three block radiuses until it forgets altogether where it came from.

Ras, my block had gardens.

Italians stuck bits of sticks in their suitcases, tucked seeds into their trunks and here they bloomed into cardoon and cucuzza

   And fig trees

Hostile climates were no match, we'd wrap them in burlap or bury them in the dirt and at the end of even the harshest winter, they'd survive.

They'd survive.

Clove Lakes Park

If four-leaf clovers are lucky
Then Clove Lakes Park is gold at the end of a rainbow
The victory on a boulevard of childhood

If I could bottle up a scent, it would be
Sunburnt-rubber-swing, tar-melt-asphalt

We are told not to stare at the sun
But I stare boldly
At the metal slide
Do not fear blindness or scalded thighs

Somehow, we are impenetrable
Children
Nothing can touch us
Not the heat, not death, or the world's cruelness

We climb upon statues in the park, become kings and queens of the
    mountain
Go to war against the armies of pigeons and swans, run them from
    the lawns

We watch the older girls smoke cigarettes and file their French
Manicured hands
While the boys play basketball
We blush at their naked chests and hair and giggle, steal glances
    anyway
We want to become part of their game

One day the sun will grow too hot, we will be too old to fit in the swing
Our thighs will sizzle at the sting of hurt
        We will stare longingly at all the small faces and how they
           Have not yet learned to be afraid

We will crush cigarette butts and leave them to clog the sewer drain
Hope those boys won't notice us, won't catcall out to us
No longer a fan of that game

I run downhill and wish for wings
That swoop out like that swan on the lake
For his long strides beside me on the way
To the drugstore as I count the cracks in sidewalks

I don't know of objects to be lucky
But I know of places I'm lucky to call home

For the ways in which they hold our ghosts

I am told a home is just
Foundation, windows, doors, and paint
But I knew then as a child
Home to be the embrace

The paint peels in corners of this house
        Fades like memory at the passing of time
I catch glimpses of a girl sometimes
Little queen of Clove Lakes Park.

Acknowledgments

Thank you to the editors and teams of the following magazines and journals that first took a chance on these poems and gave me the confidence to continue with this project.

"Things I've Heard While Growing up Italian," previously published on *The Opiate* (theopiatemagazine.com), November 2019.

"Cleaning Ceremonies," previously published in *The Opiate*, Winter 2020, Issue 20.

"The Sexiness in the Heat of Summer," previously published on *Rebelle Society*, 2019.

"Filomena, Mildred, Angelina, Alice, Michele," previously published as "Philomena, Mildred, Angelina, Alice, Michele" in *Steam Ticket*, Volume 23, 2020.

"All I Hold in My Hands," previously published in *Penumbra Literary and Art Journal*, Volume 30, 2020.

"Abraham's Antonym," previously published on *Poydras Review*, 2020.

"A Woman Holds A Vacancy" and "I Think the Dead Are Watching Me," previously published in *Press Pause Press*, Volume 6, 2022.

"Apollo," previously published in *Evening Street Review*, Number 36, Winter 2022.

"Store Brand Numerology," previously published in *Soundings East*, Volume 44, 2022.

"Clove Lakes Park," previously published on *Apricity Magazine*, 2022.

"Inaccurate Histories," previously published in *Corpus Callosum Press: Plainsongs*, Summer 2022.

"Cerebral by Nature," previously published on *A Thin Slice of Anxiety*, 2022.

"No One Covered the Fig Tree," previously published in *Poetry Bus Press*, Issue 11, 2023.

"Coffee Breaks and Familial Aches," previously published in *Narrative Northeast*, Issue 11: *Spoken Word and More*, January 4, 2024.

"Smoked Herring for Breakfast," previously published in *Big Muddy*, Volume 24, Spring 2024.

"The Old Block" and "Dustsceawung" previously published in *The Opiate*, Volume 40, Winter 2025.

"Beauty Mark or Blemish" previously published on *The Opiate* website (theopiatemagazine.com), December 2024.

A special thank you to TJ McGowan, my happy thing, for suggesting the order of these poems and helping me determine what this manuscript was really trying to say. Thank you for always holding space for me.

Thank you to the workshops led by Amy Meng, Linda Ravenswood, Stephanie Berger, and Holy Crow, and to the poetry groups where these poems first took shape—especially to my Barnegat Poetry Family. Mike Lowenberg, thank you for the title *"Abraham's Antonym."* Michael Paul Thomas, thank you for teaching me how to write a villanelle!

Thank you to *Burnt Tavern*, whose impromptu composition at the Green Planet Coffee Co. Poetry Jam provided me the musical soundscape to create *Only In Dreams Now*. I am forever grateful for this collaboration, which can be viewed on their Instagram @burnttavern.

Gratitude also goes to Tennessee Williams' *The Rose Tattoo*. The Marisa Tomei-led Broadway production in 2019 stirred something so profound in me that the opening poem was partly constructed during intermission and later finished in my hotel room, inspiring the framework of this collection.

To Alice at Golden Dragonfly, you've not only taken the chance on my work a second time, but created a home of sorts for me to feel seen and heard. I will always be grateful for what you've built and for allowing me to be a part of it.

And to my family, I don't know how to acknowledge all our hits and misses in a liner note—the love, frustration, hurt, and pain—but I hope these poems suffice. I hope they heal something in us, and I hope they showcase a love that often goes unspoken. Because it is love I have, always.

Lastly, this book is dedicated to the house my grandpa built at 104 Seneca Avenue and all the cherished childhood memories built for me there, still echoing from that kitchen down the hall.

And you, yes you, thank you for reading. I hope these poems heal you too.

www.ingramcontent.com/pod-product-compliance
Lightning Source LLC
Chambersburg PA
CBHW050903120626
46554CB00003B/982